Simply Youth Ministry
26981 Vista Terrace, Unit C
Lake Forest, CA 92630

www.simplyyouthministry.com
www.simplyjuniorhigh.com

ISBN 978-0-7644-6281-8

Printed in the United States of America

INTRODUCTION

I'll admit it; sometimes people make fun of me for getting excited about stuff. Like a fresh tap of Diet Pepsi at Taco Bell. Or getting Chick-fil-A. Or… why are all these about food?

Anyway, one thing that always gets me excited is when teenagers take up the challenge of making more of their faith. And there's no better way I know of doing that then reading the Bible on a regular basis.

That's exactly why we put together the 10 Minute Moment journals. So that you can get a "quick fix" of the best medicine to fight against a culture that's trying to bring you down and connect back with God.

I know sometimes it can be hard to find 10 minutes in your day, every day. But I promise you that if you make the effort for one month, it'll pay off. You'll experience God in a new way. One that will keep you coming back for more.

Keep growing,

Doug Fields

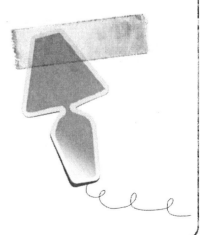

DAY 1:
EVERYTHING IS SPIRITUAL

A lot of people tend to think the world divides neatly into two categories: things that are "spiritual" and things that aren't. Going to church is spiritual; going to a basketball game is not. Reading the Bible is spiritual; watching a movie is not. It's all based on the belief that there's an invisible line cutting through our lives: On one side is the stuff God cares about, and on the other is the stuff He doesn't care about. But is that really true?

2 MINUTES

Read the passages several times (as many times as you can in 2 minutes).

1 Corinthians 10:31
So whether you eat or drink, or whatever you do, do it all for the glory of God.

Colossians 3:17
And whatever you do or say, do it as a representative of the Lord Jesus, giving thanks through him to God the Father.

1 Peter 4:10-11
10God has given each of you a gift from his great variety of spiritual gifts. Use them well to serve one another. 11Do you have the gift of speaking? Then speak as though God himself were speaking through you. Do you have the gift of helping others? Do it with all the strength and energy that God supplies. Then everything you do will bring glory to God through Jesus Christ. All glory and power to him forever and ever! Amen.

5 MINUTES

Think about the following questions and how they might apply to your life.

- The Colossians verse says we can do everything as a "representative of the Lord Jesus." In politics, a representative is someone who acts on behalf of the group of people he represents. How are we like that for Jesus?

- How is acting like a representative different than being "religious"?

- What do the Colossians verse and the Corinthians verse say about the idea of there being "spiritual" things and "unspiritual" things?

- What do the verses in Peter say we should do with the gifts God has given us?

- What are some gifts God has given YOU? How can you use them so that "God will be given the glory"?

3 MINUTES

Spend three minutes talking to God. Here are some things to talk to Him about today.

- Talk to Jesus about how you want to be a "representative" for Him. Ask Him to help you think of ways you could do that better.

- Are there areas of your life that you've kept Jesus out of because they aren't "spiritual"? Pick one area of your life you know Jesus would want to change, and ask for His help in giving that area of your life to Him.

- Ask Jesus to show you people who need to see Him today. Ask Him to show you ways that you can represent Jesus to these people.

THOUGHTS

This space is here for you to jot down some thoughts, write out a prayer, draw a picture, or do whatever you want to help you remember your 10-minute moment.

DAY 2:
WE WERE SINNERS...

There's an old saying within Christianity that goes something like this: "I'm just a sinner, saved by grace." The idea being that we once were completely separate from God because we'd disobeyed (that's the sinner part) but then Jesus did something for us we didn't deserve (that's the grace part) and now we don't have to be separated from God anymore — both now and for eternity. Awesome, huh? The problem is that people who talk about being a "sinner saved by grace" think we're still separated from God. But that's not what the Bible says...

Read the passage several times (as many times as you can in 2 minutes).

Romans 6:6-11

6We know that our old sinful selves were crucified with Christ so that sin might lose its power in our lives. We are no longer slaves to sin. 7For when we died with Christ we were set free from the power of sin. 8And since we died with Christ, we know we will also live with him. 9We are sure of this because Christ was raised from the dead, and he will never die again. Death no longer has any power over him. 10When he died, he died once to break the power of sin. But now that he lives, he lives for the glory of God. 11So you also should consider yourselves to be dead to the power of sin and alive to God through Christ Jesus.

5 MINUTES

Think about the following questions and how they might apply to your life.

- What does vs. 6 say happened to "our old sinful selves"?

- What does vs. 7 say we are free from?

- What does vs. 11 say we should be able to do now?

- Why do you think it's important to know we are free from sin? How is this better than thinking we're still "sinners."

- A lot of times we tend to think of worship — which just means doing things for God instead of for us — as something that's unnatural. It feels like everything in us wants to do what's wrong. Why do you think we feel that way? How does Romans 6:6-11 help us be better "God-worshippers"?

3 MINUTES

Spend three minutes talking to God. Here are some things to talk to Him about today.

- Almost all Christians — and probably you too — struggle with understanding that they are FREE of sin. We don't worship God well because we don't understand that worshipping is our new IDENTITY. Ask God to help you see yourself the way He does.

- A lot of us believe lies about ourselves. That we are basically bad, flawed, or unlovable. Ask God to remove any lies that have built up in your life.

- Ask God for His help over the next 24 hours to realize that He's always with you. Tell Him you want to learn how to live life constantly worshipping Him.

THOUGHTS

This space is here for you to jot down some thoughts, write out a prayer, draw a picture, or do whatever you want to help you remember your 10-minute moment.

DAY 3:
LIFE FROM 35,000 FEET

If you've had a window seat when flying somewhere you know how different the world looks from 35,000 feet up. Houses are specks. Neighborhoods are swallowed up by cities. Cities become islands in the middle of unpopulated land. Whenever we can see the big picture of our lives, everything looks different. Now imagine if we could see our lives from GOD'S perspective...

2 MINUTES

Read the passage several times (as many times as you can in 2 minutes).

Colossians 3:1-4

¹Since you have been raised to new life with Christ, set your sights on the realities of heaven, where Christ sits in the place of honor at God's right hand. ²Think about the things of heaven, not the things of earth. ³For you died to this life, and your real life is hidden with Christ in God. ⁴And when Christ, who is your life, is revealed to the whole world, you will share in all his glory.

5 MINUTES

Think about the following questions and how they might apply to your life.

- In vs. 1 it says "set your sights on the reality of heaven." What do you think that means? What ARE the realities of heaven?

11

Imagine that you die and go to heaven, and you and Jesus are looking back on your life…

- Write 3 things in your life right now you'll be proud of:

- Write 3 things in your life you'll wish you'd done differently:

- What do you think it means in vs. 3 when it says "your real life is hidden with Christ in God"?

The truth is that it's really easy to live each day seeing things from ground level. And because of that we waste our time — or make poor decisions — that one day we'll regret. Part of worship is learning to see things from God's perspective and believing that His way is best.

3 MINUTES

Spend three minutes talking to God. Here are some things to talk to Him about today.

- Look at the three areas in your life you think you'll be proud of someday. Spend time talking with God about those areas. Ask God to help you realize how PROUD He is of you for doing well in those areas.

- Look at the three areas in your life that aren't so good. Ask God to help you see those from His perspective, and REALLY BELIEVE His way of seeing it is the right way.

THOUGHTS

This space is here for you to jot down some thoughts, write out a prayer, draw a picture, or do whatever you want to help you remember your 10-minute moment.

DAY 4:
HIS FAITHFUL LOVE ENDURES FOREVER
(REPEAT 90X)

Just a little bit of honesty here. "Being grateful" isn't really my strong suit. I know I should be, but I tend to be the kind of guy who's always complaining (out loud or in my head) about how things aren't as good as they should be. Which is why the Scriptures below really put me in my place. When I'm constantly being thankful, I'm killing selfishness and replacing it with thankfulness to God. Sometimes the most worshipful thing we can do is just tell God "Thanks!"

2 MINUTES

Read the passages several times (as many times as you can in 2 minutes).

Ephesians 5:20
And give thanks for everything to God the Father in the name of our Lord Jesus Christ.

Psalm 136
¹ Give thanks to the LORD, for he is good! His faithful love endures forever.
² Give thanks to the God of gods. His faithful love endures forever.
³ Give thanks to the Lord of lords. His faithful love endures forever.
⁴ Give thanks to him who alone does mighty miracles. His faithful love endures forever.
⁵ Give thanks to him who made the heavens so skillfully. His faithful love endures forever.
⁶ Give thanks to him who placed the earth among the waters. His faithful love endures forever.
⁷ Give thanks to him who made the heavenly lights—His faithful love endures forever.
⁸ the sun to rule the day, His faithful love endures forever.
⁹ and the moon and stars to rule the night. His faithful love endures forever.

¹⁰ *Give thanks to him who killed the firstborn of Egypt. His faithful love endures forever.*

¹¹ *He brought Israel out of Egypt. His faithful love endures forever.*

¹² *He acted with a strong hand and powerful arm. His faithful love endures forever.*

¹³ *Give thanks to him who parted the Red Sea. His faithful love endures forever.*

¹⁴ *He led Israel safely through, His faithful love endures forever.*

¹⁵ *but he hurled Pharaoh and his army into the Red Sea. His faithful love endures forever.*

¹⁶ *Give thanks to him who led his people through the wilderness. His faithful love endures forever.*

¹⁷ *Give thanks to him who struck down mighty kings. His faithful love endures forever.*

¹⁸ *He killed powerful kings—His faithful love endures forever.*

¹⁹ *Sihon king of the Amorites, His faithful love endures forever.*

²⁰ *and Og king of Bashan. His faithful love endures forever.*

²¹ *God gave the land of these kings as an inheritance—His faithful love endures forever.*

²² *a special possession to his servant Israel. His faithful love endures forever.*

²³ *He remembered us in our weakness. His faithful love endures forever.*

²⁴ *He saved us from our enemies. His faithful love endures forever.*

²⁵ *He gives food to every living thing. His faithful love endures forever.*

²⁶ *Give thanks to the God of heaven. His faithful love endures forever.*

5 MINUTES

Think about the following questions and how they might apply to your life.

- What does the verse in Ephesians 5 say we should be grateful for?

- Is being grateful to God something that comes easy for you, or is it hard? How do you think someone becomes "more grateful"? How does the (stinking LONG!) passage from Psalm 136 help answer how we can be grateful?

Psalm 136 is basically the country of Israel looking back through its history — starting at creation — and saying "thanks God!"

- What are some things in nature you are grateful for?

- What are some things in your past you are grateful for? (Examples: family, friends, protection from harm, ways you can see God guiding your life.)

- What are some things in your life TODAY you are thankful for?

- What are some qualities about God you are thankful for?

3 MINUTES

Spend three minutes talking to God. Here are some things to talk to Him about today.

- Spend time looking over this list you've just created. Thank God for everything you wrote down. Think about how God thought up each one of those things. He didn't just ALLOW them to happen; He CREATED them!

- Think about some things in your life you are angry or bitter or frustrated about. Ask God to help you learn how to be thankful even in the middle of bad stuff.

THOUGHTS

This space is here for you to jot down some thoughts, write out a prayer, draw a picture, or do whatever you want to help you remember your 10-minute moment.

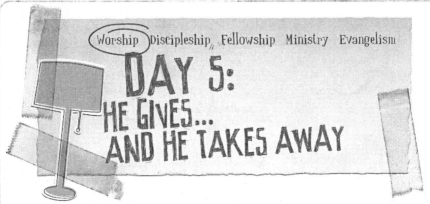

DAY 5:
HE GIVES...
AND HE TAKES AWAY

It's easy to worship God (do things for Him, not for us) when life is good, right? It's easy to worship Him when a talented praise band is playing a worship song we like. During day 4 we talked about worshipping God for everything He's given. But what about when He "takes away"?

2 MINUTES

Read the passage several times (as many times as you can in 2 minutes).

Job 1:1
There once was a man named Job who lived in the land of Uz. He was blameless—a man of complete integrity. He feared God and stayed away from evil.

Job 1:6-22
⁶One day the members of the heavenly court came to present themselves before the LORD, and the Accuser, Satan, came with them. ⁷"Where have you come from?" the LORD asked Satan.

Satan answered the LORD, "I have been patrolling the earth, watching everything that's going on."

⁸Then the LORD asked Satan, "Have you noticed my servant Job? He is the finest man in all the earth. He is blameless—a man of complete integrity. He fears God and stays away from evil."

⁹Satan replied to the LORD, "Yes, but Job has good reason to fear God. ¹⁰You have always put a wall of protection around him and his home and his property. You have made him prosper in everything he does. Look how rich he is! *11*But reach out and take away everything he has, and he will surely curse you to your face!"

12"All right, you may test him," the LORD said to Satan. "Do whatever you want with everything he possesses, but don't harm him physically." So Satan left the LORD's presence.

*13*One day when Job's sons and daughters were feasting at the oldest brother's house, *14*a messenger arrived at Job's home with this news: "Your oxen were plowing, with the donkeys feeding beside them, *15*when the Sabeans raided us. They stole all the animals and killed all the farmhands. I am the only one who escaped to tell you."

*16*While he was still speaking, another messenger arrived with this news: "The fire of God has fallen from heaven and burned up your sheep and all the shepherds. I am the only one who escaped to tell you."

*17*While he was still speaking, a third messenger arrived with this news: "Three bands of Chaldean raiders have stolen your camels and killed your servants. I am the only one who escaped to tell you."

*18*While he was still speaking, another messenger arrived with this news: "Your sons and daughters were feasting in their oldest brother's home. *19*Suddenly, a powerful wind swept in from the wilderness and hit the house on all sides. The house collapsed, and all your children are dead. I am the only one who escaped to tell you."

*20*Job stood up and tore his robe in grief. Then he shaved his head and fell to the ground to worship. *21*He said, "I came naked from my mother's womb, and I will be naked when I leave. The LORD gave me what I had, and the LORD has taken it away. Praise the name of the LORD!"

*22*In all of this, Job did not sin by blaming God.

5 MINUTES

Think about the following questions and how they might apply to your life.

- Make a list of the ways vs. 1 describes Job. Now make a list of the ways God describes Job in vs. 8.

- If Job was such a great, God-fearing guy, why did God let so much bad stuff happen to him? (This is a REALLY tough question to answer. Don't worry about coming up with a "perfect answer." Just think about it.)

- If you lost your family and all your possessions in one day, how would you respond? How does Job respond in vs. 20-22? How is Job's response a form of worship?

The truth is that Job never gets an answer as to why God let such horrible stuff happen ... and neither do we as the reader. One of the hardest things about being a Christian is that sometimes we don't KNOW why bad things happen. But God promises to take ALL things — even really awful things — and make something good out of them. Part of worship is believing this even when we're confused, hurt, or overwhelmed.

3 MINUTES

Spend three minutes talking to God. Here are some things to talk to Him about today.

- How does the story of Job make you feel about God? Whatever your reaction is, tell Him about it.

- Is there something in your life that you are mad at God about? Be honest about it. He knows anyway.

- If you are currently hurting, ask God 1) to help you know that He loves you and is close by and 2) to help you trust that He will work something good out of the bad.

THOUGHTS

This space is here for you to jot down some thoughts, write out a prayer, draw a picture, or do whatever you want to help you remember your 10-minute moment.

DAY 6:
HOW HE LOVES US

There's this nasty tendency as a Christian to make things really complicated. Life gets busy and stressful and out-of-control, and we start freaking out. And then we feel like spiritual failures, so we try really, really hard to do all the right things for God — because that's worship right? — and we start feeling like we're spending all our energy TRYING to be good rather than just loving God. Sometimes it's good to step back and just focus on one truth. Jesus loves you. You. Jesus loves you. HE loves YOU.

4 MINUTES

Read the passages several times (as many times as you can in 4 minutes).

John 3:16
For God loved the world so much that he gave his one and only Son, so that everyone who believes in him will not perish but have eternal life.

Romans 5:8
But God showed his great love for us by sending Christ to die for us while we were still sinners.

1 John 4:9-10
⁹God showed how much he loved us by sending his one and only Son into the world so that we might have eternal life through him. ¹⁰This is real love—not that we loved God, but that he loved us and sent his Son as a sacrifice to take away our sins.

0 MINUTES

Think about the following questions and how they might apply to your life (there are no questions to answer today — spend the extra time talking to God!).

6 MINUTES

Spend six minutes talking to God. Here are some things to talk to Him about today.

- Worship only makes sense in a relationship. We can only really worship God when we are in relationship with Him. Ask God today to help you feel His love in a new, personal, amazing, intimate way.

- What do you think are some of the things that get in the way of you feeling God's presence? It could be stress from school, a job, your family. It could be pain from someone who has hurt you. It could be bitterness or resentment. Maybe you've allowed disobedience to sneak in to your life. Ask Him for help in removing these obstacles.

- Read John 3:16 again. Ask God to make some part of this verse stand out in a new way to you. If you want, write out the verse using your own words.

- Spend at least 1 minute being completely quiet. During this time tell God you want to hear whatever it is He wants to say. He may speak to you, or He may not. The point is that you listened!

- Ask God to help you share His love with others today.

you can write your thoughts on the next page

THOUGHTS

This space is here for you to jot down some thoughts, write out a prayer, draw a picture, or do whatever you want to help you remember your 10-minute moment.

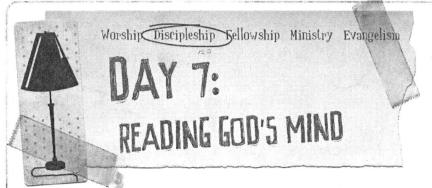

DAY 7:
READING GOD'S MIND

A lot of times we think of God as being hard to know. Sure, we imagine Him loving us (in some vague way). And we're pretty sure He wants us to be good. But in terms of what He's thinking right now — who knows! In terms of His plan for our lives right now, we just kind of hope that if we keep trying to be good then everything will work out. But what if God's plan for us was better than that?

2 MINUTES

Read the passage several times (as many times as you can in 2 minutes).

1 Corinthians 2:9-12
⁹That is what the Scriptures mean when they say,

"No eye has seen, no ear has heard, and no mind has imagined what God has prepared for those who love him."

¹⁰But it was to us that God revealed these things by his Spirit. For his Spirit searches out everything and shows us God's deep secrets. ¹¹No one can know a person's thoughts except that person's own spirit, and no one can know God's thoughts except God's own Spirit. ¹²And we have received God's Spirit (not the world's spirit), so we can know the wonderful things God has freely given us.

5 MINUTES

Think about the following questions and how they might apply to your life.

- Look again at vs. 9. What does this verse say "no mind has imagined"?

- Again in vs. 9, who is God's plan for?

- According to vs. 10, what can we now know? According to vs. 11, how come we can know God's plan for our lives now?

- It seems like God is REALLY interested in our discovering His plan for our lives. Why, then, do you think we have such a hard time figuring it out?

Spend three minutes talking to God. Here are some things to talk to Him about today.

- According to 1 Corinthians, God's Spirit — His actual presence — dwells IN everyone who is a Christ-follower. This might seem weird, but spend some time talking to the Spirit of God (the Holy Spirit) who dwells inside you. This is the same thing as talking to God, really. But sometimes it feels different to think of God as dwelling IN us. Ask the Holy Spirit for guidance and help in an area of life you are confused about or struggling with.

- Pray about some of the things you think might be keeping you from hearing God's voice speaking to you. If it's something in your life that you know isn't part of God's plan for you, talk to Him about that. Tell Him you want that area to change.

- Ask God's Spirit in you (remember, this is the same thing as talking to God) to help you walk throughout today listening to Him.

THOUGHTS

This space is here for you to jot down some thoughts, write out a prayer, draw a picture, or do whatever you want to help you remember your 10-minute moment.

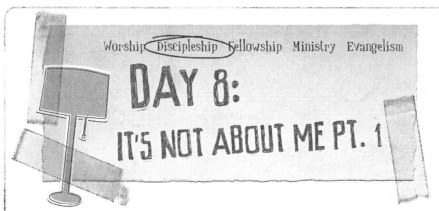

DAY 8:
IT'S NOT ABOUT ME PT. 1

It's sometimes easy to think that God exists kind of like the genie from the movie "Aladdin." Whenever we need Him we rub the magic lamp (prayer) and out pops God to fulfill our wishes. But all of us know, deep down, that if God really IS the one who created everything then He probably doesn't exist to do whatever we want. As a matter of fact, we'll never grow spiritually until we accept the fact that He's in charge — not us.

2 MINUTES

Read the passages several times (as many times as you can in 2 minutes).

Matthew 16:24-25
²⁴Then Jesus said to his disciples, "If any of you wants to be my follower, you must turn from your selfish ways, take up your cross, and follow me. ²⁵If you try to hang on to your life, you will lose it. But if you give up your life for my sake, you will save it."

Matthew 6:24
"No one can serve two masters. For you will hate one and love the other; you will be devoted to one and despise the other. You cannot serve both God and money."

5 MINUTES

Think about the following questions and how they might apply to your life.

- In Matthew 16:24 what do you think the phrase "selfish ambition" means?

28

- Why does vs. 24 say we have to put aside the selfish things if we want to follow God? Do you think this is true? Why can't we serve both?

- What do you think it means to "shoulder your cross"? What was a cross back then? How is following Jesus like crucifixion?

- If following Jesus is about "dying to ourselves," what does that mean practically for you, today? What is one thing in your life that you know needs to be crucified?

3 MINUTES

Spend three minutes talking to God. Here are some things to talk to Him about today.

- First off, think about how Jesus literally picked up a cross and died and then rose again for you. Remembering that He's actually right with you (and His Spirit is in you), thank Him for what He did for you. Ask Him to make what He did something very real to you, not just something you've read about.

- Second, pray for the areas in your life that you know need to be "crucified." Ask God, in His power, to kill those things in your life. Remembering that it's His power working through you, ask God to give you the strength to be obedient to Him today.

- Finally, tell God that you want to grow spiritually today. Ask Him to give you wisdom to see what needs to be done and the power to do it.

you can write your thoughts →
on the next page

THOUGHTS

This space is here for you to jot down some thoughts, write out a prayer, draw a picture, or do whatever you want to help you remember your 10-minute moment.

DAY 9:
GIVE US LIBERTY...

Sometimes God's rules feel REALLY restrictive, right? I mean, how much stuff do people around you get away with — and feel perfectly okay with — that you're not supposed to do? There's the big stuff: hooking up, having sex, going to parties, or getting drunk. There's the "small" stuff: cussing, gossiping, disobeying parents, stealing, or lying. Honestly, sometimes following Jesus feels like losing all your freedom. But is that true? Is growing as a disciple in Christ really worth it?

2 MINUTES

Read the passages several times (as many times as you can in 2 minutes).

John 8:31-32
[31]*Jesus said to the people who believed in him, "You are truly my disciples if you remain faithful to my teachings. [32]And you will know the truth, and the truth will set you free."*

Romans 6:7
For when we died with Christ we were set free from the power of sin.

1 Peter 5:8
Stay alert! Watch out for your great enemy, the devil. He prowls around like a roaring lion, looking for someone to devour.

5 MINUTES

Think about the following questions and how they might apply to your life.

- According to John 8:31, who are Jesus' real disciples? What do you think "fake" disciples look like?

- Jesus says that if we learn what He says and obey it, that it will "set us free." What do you think that means? Free from what?

- According to Romans 6:7, what were people who became Christ-followers set free from? HOW were we set free?

- What do you think it means to be free from sin?

- According to 1 Peter 5:8, who "prowls around" for us? Considering this verse, WHO do you think God's rules free us from?

- What's one area of your life where you struggle to live as Jesus' disciple and be free from Satan's lies?

3 MINUTES

Spend three minutes talking to God. Here are some things to talk to Him about today.

- Jesus died so that you could be free. Spend some time thanking Him for that. Also, ask Him to help you stay obedient to Him today so that you can STAY in that freedom.

- The Bible says Satan's like a lion looking to kill people. But it ALSO says we've been freed from him and don't have to fear him anymore. This might seem weird, but ask Jesus to protect you today from Satan's lies.

- Talk to God for a couple minutes about any prayer requests, concerns, or stresses in your life right now. Remember, He LIKES talking to you!

THOUGHTS

This space is here for you to jot down some thoughts, write out a prayer, draw a picture, or do whatever you want to help you remember your 10-minute moment.

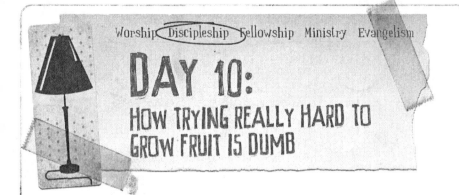

DAY 10:
HOW TRYING REALLY HARD TO GROW FRUIT IS DUMB

Has there ever been a more boring word than "discipleship"? I mean, if you know what it actually means (being an every-second student of Jesus) it's kind of cool. But if we're honest, most of us hear the word and either stifle a yawn or an unpleasant shudder. I believe the reason for this is that when we think of discipleship, we also think of the word "discipline." And discipline sounds like trying really hard to do something I hate doing. (Is this just me?) Is this all "growing in Jesus" means?

2 MINUTES

Read the passage several times (as many times as you can in 2 minutes).

John 15:5-10

⁵"Yes, I am the vine; you are the branches. Those who remain in me, and I in them, will produce much fruit. For apart from me you can do nothing. ⁶Anyone who does not remain in me is thrown away like a useless branch and withers. Such branches are gathered into a pile to be burned. ⁷But if you remain in me and my words remain in you, you may ask for anything you want, and it will be granted! ⁸When you produce much fruit, you are my true disciples. This brings great glory to my Father.

⁹"I have loved you even as the Father has loved me. Remain in my love. ¹⁰When you obey my commandments, you remain in my love, just as I obey my Father's commandments and remain in his love.

5 MINUTES

Think about the following questions and how they might apply to your life.

- There's a phrase that shows up in nearly every verse from this passage. What is it?

- What do you think this phrase means?

- What example does Jesus use in vs. 5? Which part of the tree are we?

- We all know that being a Christian means becoming a certain kind of person — but according to these verses, how do we become that kind of person?

- How is "remaining in Jesus" different than "trying really hard"?

Here's the truth: YOU don't make yourself into the person God wants you to be. HE does that. So what role do we have in that process? We stay connected to Him. And then when life gets difficult we lean on Him to make us the kind of person who gets through it.

3 MINUTES

Spend three minutes talking to God. Here are some things to talk to Him about today.

- God wants you to be in relationship with Him 24/7. So ask Him to help you do that. Tell Him that if there's anything He wants to say, you're listening — then wait for a couple minutes.

- Pray that God would reveal ways that you can help show someone who doesn't know Jesus see His love today.

you can write your thoughts on the next page

THOUGHTS

This space is here for you to jot down some thoughts, write out a prayer, draw a picture, or do whatever you want to help you remember your 10-minute moment.

DAY 11:
THE MORE YOU KNOW

If there's one thing most teenagers hate, it's a reading assignment. You might even LOVE reading, but the moment a teacher tells you that you HAVE to read it, you think, "I'm not doing that!" This is true sometimes with the Bible. We're not opposed to reading it — in theory — but feeling like we're SUPPOSED to read it can make us think, "I'm not doing that!" But if the Bible really IS God's love letter to us, maybe we should think about it differently. Maybe we might even (gasp!) grow to like reading it!

2 MINUTES

Read the passage several times (as many times as you can in 2 minutes).

2 Timothy 3:15-17

15You have been taught the holy Scriptures from childhood, and they have given you the wisdom to receive the salvation that comes by trusting in Christ Jesus. 16All Scripture is inspired by God and is useful to teach us what is true and to make us realize what is wrong in our lives. It corrects us when we are wrong and teaches us to do what is right. 17God uses it to prepare and equip his people to do every good work.

5 MINUTES

Think about the following questions and how they might apply to your life.

- This book, which is written to a young pastor named Timothy, says he has been "taught the holy Scriptures from childhood." Have you grown up being taught the Bible?

- If so, do you sometimes struggle with feeling like you've heard this all before? What do you do about that?

- Why does vs. 15 say God's Word to us (the Bible) is important? What does vs. 16 say about its importance?

- What do you think it means that the Scriptures are "inspired by God?" (If you don't know, but you're really feeling studious, look up the word "inspired" in the dictionary.)

- According to v. 17, what's the importance of the Scriptures?

3 MINUTES

Spend three minutes talking to God. Here are some things to talk to Him about today.

- Talk to God about the Bible. If you LOVE reading it, thank Him for it. If — like most people — it's kind of hard for you to read it sometimes, ask Him for help. Specifically, ask God to give you a desire to read it. He LOVES when you ask for His help.

- Ask God to help you understand what you're reading in the Bible, from this time forward. This would actually be a good thing to pray every time you go to read it!

- Spend some time talking to God about whatever is on your mind today.

THOUGHTS

This space is here for you to jot down some thoughts, write out a prayer, draw a picture, or do whatever you want to help you remember your 10-minute moment.

DAY 12:
THIS IS YOUR BRAIN ON GOD

So there were these crazy commercials a few years back — you may have seen them — that showed a normal egg and said, "This is your brain." Then they'd crack the egg over a sizzling skillet. The yolk would immediately start frying, and the announcer would say, "This is your brain on drugs. Any questions?" I mention this because if we're really going to grow to be more like Jesus, we have to stop frying our brains. Seriously. So much of the stuff we watch, listen to, read, and talk about fries our brain to the point where we can't think of things the way God does. But it doesn't have to be like that.

2 MINUTES

Read the passage several times (as many times as you can in 2 minutes).

Philippians 4:8
And now, dear brothers and sisters, one final thing. Fix your thoughts on what is true, and honorable, and right, and pure, and lovely, and admirable. Think about things that are excellent and worthy of praise.

5 MINUTES

Think about the following questions and how they might apply to your life.

- This verse lists eight different characteristics of the things we should fill our lives with. Which words stand out to you? What do you think they mean?

- Make a quick list of TV shows you watch, bands you listen to, or books you read. How many of them fit the words from this verse? (Note: Just because something isn't obviously labeled "Christian" doesn't mean it is or isn't healthy. Honestly evaluate the effect these things have on you.)

- Think about your conversations. What conversations do you have that don't qualify as being true, honorable, pure, or worthy of praise? Is there a specific area where you seem to say or do things that don't fall into this category?

- This verse isn't about what we DON'T do. It's more about what we DO. What are things in your life that DO fit this verse? What are things in your life that you could add that fit this verse?

3 MINUTES

Spend three minutes talking to God. Here are some things to talk to Him about today.

- I hope God spoke to you through today's devotional, which means you probably know what you need to talk about. Pray about the bad stuff and tell Him you want to do more of the good stuff. Know that God is mostly concerned with the kind of person you're becoming. Talk to Him about how you want to belong to Him. Ask for help "unscrambling" the parts of your brain that don't think in a healthy way.

*you can write your thoughts ——>
on the next page*

THOUGHTS

This space is here for you to jot down some thoughts, write out a prayer, draw a picture, or do whatever you want to help you remember your 10-minute moment.

DAY 13:
UNITED, WE STAND

We know that we need other people. Everyone knows that. No one really likes to be alone for very long. In fact, people who are isolated from others for TOO long tend to go crazy. (Ever seen the movie "Cast Away"?) And so in school people join teams and form clubs and are part of cliques. They hang out in groups or go on dates. People being with people is normal. So why, as Christians, do we sometimes isolate ourselves?

2 MINUTES

Read the passage several times (as many times as you can in 2 minutes).

Hebrews 10:23-25
23Let us hold tightly without wavering to the hope we affirm, for God can be trusted to keep his promise. 24Let us think of ways to motivate one another to acts of love and good works. 25And let us not neglect our meeting together, as some people do, but encourage one another, especially now that the day of his return is drawing near.

5 MINUTES

Think about the following questions and how they might apply to your life.

- Vs. 24 says, "motivate one another to acts of love and good works." Think through a normal day. Do your actions encourage others around you to be more loving or selfless?

Do your closest friends encourage YOU to be more loving or selfless?

- Vs. 25 says, "let us not neglect our meeting together." Why do you think it's so important for Christians to meet together regularly? What would some of the consequences be if we didn't?

- Think through the people you surround yourself with. Do your closest friends point you toward Jesus or away from Him? If away, do you see that as being a problem, or do you think you're okay?

- Is there a regular time in your week when you hang out with other Christians to talk about Jesus? Is this an area where you need to improve, or do you think you're doing pretty well?

3 MINUTES

Spend three minutes talking to God. Here are some things to talk to Him about today.

- Today's passage seems to take this struggle we're in as Christians pretty seriously. Pray that God would open your eyes to temptation and sin today and help you fight against it.

- If you have friends in your life who point you toward Jesus, thank God for them and pray for them today. If you don't have people like this, ask God to put someone like that in your life.

- Ask God to help you be an encouragement to other people today. Ask Him to show you ways you can "motivate one another to acts of love and good works."

THOUGHTS

This space is here for you to jot down some thoughts, write out a prayer, draw a picture, or do whatever you want to help you remember your 10-minute moment.

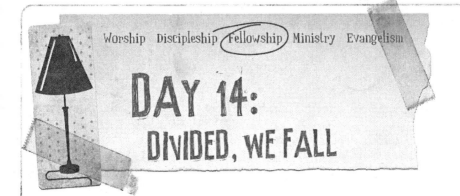

DAY 14:
DIVIDED, WE FALL

On the TV show "Lost," one of the main characters — a guy named Jack — uttered a phrase that would become famous throughout the run of the show: "We can either live together, or die alone." Now, we don't live on a freaky island that makes us see dead people or that has smoke monsters (yep, both from the show), but we DO live in a world where it's tough to honor Jesus. You might remember that Satan, our enemy, is like a lion out hunting his prey (us). So what do we do as Christians? Well … we live together, or die alone.

2 MINUTES

Read the passage several times (as many times as you can in 2 minutes).

Ecclesiastes 4:9-12
9 Two people are better off than one, for they can help each other succeed. 10 If one person falls, the other can reach out and help. But someone who falls alone is in real trouble. 11 Likewise, two people lying close together can keep each other warm. But how can one be warm alone? 12 A person standing alone can be attacked and defeated, but two can stand back-to-back and conquer. Three are even better, for a triple-braided cord is not easily broken.

5 MINUTES

Think about the following questions and how they might apply to your life.

- This passage from the Bible offers several illustrations of why it's better to be together than to be alone. Which one stands out to you the most? Why?

- Look specifically at vs. 12. What does it say happens to the person who fights alone? Think about your life and the struggle to be who God made you to be. Have you ever tried to "fight alone" and failed? When?

- Do you think things might have been different if you had invited another Christ-follower to help you?

- What's one area of your life right now where you're struggling? Could you ask someone you know/trust for help?

Spend three minutes talking to God. Here are some things to talk to Him about today.

- Maybe today as you were reading this, God brought up some stuff in your life that you know you need to ask others for help with (maybe a Christian friend or a youth pastor or your small group leader). Ask God for help in 1) knowing HOW to fix it and 2) having the courage to fix it.

- Do you have a friend that you know is struggling with something? Pray for that person. Ask God to show you ways you can help your friend today.

- Thank God for sending Jesus to die for you. That seems a little off-topic, but it all comes back to your relationship with God. Ask Him for help with whatever you know you're going to need today. Ask Him for help in loving Him through your actions today.

THOUGHTS

This space is here for you to jot down some thoughts, write out
a prayer, draw a picture, or do whatever you want to help you
remember your 10-minute moment.

DAY 15:
NICE BODY!

We live in a world that ranks a person's value by really stupid things. Think about it: How important is it to be a good athlete or actor? Why is being attractive (for a max of 20-30 years) a guaranteed way to get attention? But we as Christians, buy into it. Let's be honest: It's hard for us to believe that our worth isn't determined by how smart/pretty/funny/popular/athletic/well-dressed we are. There are a thousand problems with believing this, but one of the biggest is that it destroys unity with other Christians. Rather than working together to tell the world about Jesus, we fight for who's the most important! But doing that is about as dumb as poking ourselves in the eye.

2 MINUTES

Read the passage several times (as many times as you can in 2 minutes).

Romans 12:3-5

3Because of the privilege and authority God has given me, I give each of you this warning: Don't think you are better than you really are. Be honest in your evaluation of yourselves, measuring yourselves by the faith God has given us. 4Just as our bodies have many parts and each part has a special function, 5so it is with Christ's body. We are many parts of one body, and we all belong to each other.

Think about the following questions and how they might apply to your life.

- According to vs. 3, how should we measure our value? And where does it say our faith comes from?

- What are some parts of your body that are obviously important, that you know you wouldn't want to live without? What is one part of your body that isn't as obvious, but which you'd die if you didn't have?

- Is there someone in your life you're jealous of? Is there a gift/attribute that person has that you wish YOU had? If so, why do you want it so badly?

- What do you think your role in God's body is? What do you think He has created you to do?

- You're a part of the body of Christ, which means you were made to work with other parts. Who are some people in your life that you could work together with to do things for God? What could those things be?

3 MINUTES

Spend three minutes talking to God. Here are some things to talk to Him about today.

- If you're struggling with jealousy or gossip toward another Christian, admit it to God and ask Him to help you stop immediately! Admit that you're doing it because you don't feel valued. Ask God for help in getting your value/worth from Him.

- Ask God a really dangerous/fun question: "If you could use me to do anything, what would it be?" Ask Him to show you a tiny bit of the answer over the next week.

THOUGHTS

This space is here for you to jot down some thoughts, write out a prayer, draw a picture, or do whatever you want to help you remember your 10-minute moment.

DAY 16:
WHAT'S MINE, IS YOURS

We don't exactly live in a culture that's big on community. It's not uncommon to live just a few houses down from people but never meet them. Sure we have friends, classmates, and co-workers, but for the most part, we keep them at a certain distance. For instance, how many people really know some of the stuff you're struggling with the most right now? Not everyone needs to know every detail of your life — that's for sure — but God's plan for Christians is to have a community that we can depend on … for everything.

2 MINUTES

Read the passage several times (as many times as you can in 2 minutes).

Acts 4:32-37
32All the believers were united in heart and mind. And they felt that what they owned was not their own, so they shared everything they had. 33The apostles testified powerfully to the resurrection of the Lord Jesus, and God's great blessing was upon them all. 34There were no needy people among them, because those who owned land or houses would sell them 35and bring the money to the apostles to give to those in need.

36For instance, there was Joseph, the one the apostles nicknamed Barnabas (which means "Son of Encouragement"). He was from the tribe of Levi and came from the island of Cyprus. 37He sold a field he owned and brought the money to the apostles.

5 MINUTES

Think about the following questions and how they might apply to your life.

- In vs. 32, what do you think it means that "believers were united in heart and mind"? Do you see think the church you attend could be described that way? Why or why not?

- Vs. 32 also says the early Christians "felt what they owned was not their own." Why do you think they felt this way? Do you have anyone in your life to whom you could honestly say, "what's mine is yours"?

- How would the church look different if everyone "felt what they owned was not their own"?

- Vs. 34 says "there were no needy people among them." You may not have much money, but the people around you are still in need of things you possess: time, love, attention, respect, and prayer. How can you offer one of these gifts to someone today who is "poor?"

3 MINUTES

Spend three minutes talking to God. Here are some things to talk to Him about today.

- God clearly wants us to live in community with other Christians, where we look out for each other's needs. If you have Christian friends that you do life with — especially if you're in a small group — pray that God would help you see how you can serve them this week.

- If you are not a part of a regular Christian community — a small group, a youth ministry, whatever — pray that God would help you find one or meet people you can do life with.

THOUGHTS

This space is here for you to jot down some thoughts, write out a prayer, draw a picture, or do whatever you want to help you remember your 10-minute moment.

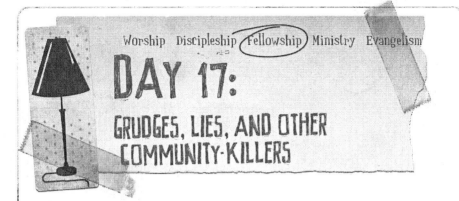

DAY 17:
GRUDGES, LIES, AND OTHER COMMUNITY-KILLERS

God wants Christians to be unified – to be of one mind and heart. So why do we spend so much of our time fighting? Why are some churches known as places where people get hurt or are excluded? It's because we don't take seriously the following verses...

2 MINUTES

Read the passage several times (as many times as you can in 2 minutes).

Ephesians 4:25-29

[25]So stop telling lies. Let us tell our neighbors the truth, for we are all parts of the same body. [26]And "don't sin by letting anger control you." Don't let the sun go down while you are still angry, [27]for anger gives a foothold to the devil.

[28]If you are a thief, quit stealing. Instead, use your hands for good hard work, and then give generously to others in need. [29]Don't use foul or abusive language. Let everything you say be good and helpful, so that your words will be an encouragement to those who hear them.

5 MINUTES

Think about the following questions and how they might apply to your life.

- Why does the Bible say Christians should tell the truth to each other? What does that mean?

- On a scale of 1-10 — with 10 being pretty much a modern-day Pinocchio — how bad are you about telling lies? Why do you do that? How does that cause problems with the people you do life with?

- Why is lying easier sometimes than telling the truth? When we lie, whose best interest are we protecting?

- This passage says "don't sin by letting anger control you." What do you think the difference is between being angry and being controlled by anger? How does the second half of vs. 26 keep that from happening?

- Why do you think Satan is so determined to keep Christians from living healthily together? Is there any way he's using you to create problems?

3 MINUTES

Spend three minutes talking to God. Here are some things to talk to Him about today.

- Some pretty obvious stuff to pray about today. If you're dealing with anger or lying, talk to God about it. Ask Him to help you see why you do that. Tell Him you know you want to stop but need His help.

- Continue to ask God to give you healthy friendships with other Christians. Pray that God would make you the kind of influence on other Christians that would help them become who God created them to be.

THOUGHTS

This space is here for you to jot down some thoughts, write out
a prayer, draw a picture, or do whatever you want to help you
remember your 10-minute moment.

DAY 18:
ONE

The Bible teaches that God is one God. One. That's it. But it also teaches that this one God exists simultaneously in three parts: God the Father, God the Son (Jesus), and God the Holy Spirit. God is not three separate gods. And Jesus and the Holy Spirit are not lesser gods. He's one God in three parts. Weird, huh? But it's also one of the coolest ideas in the Bible. And it gets even cooler when you read verses like the one below.

2 MINUTES

Read the passage several times (as many times as you can in 2 minutes).

John 17:20-23

[20]*"I am praying not only for these disciples but also for all who will ever believe in me through their message.* [21]*I pray that they will all be one, just as you and I are one—as you are in me, Father, and I am in you. And may they be in us so that the world will believe you sent me.*

[22]*"I have given them the glory you gave me, so they may be one as we are one.* [23]*I am in them and you are in me. May they experience such perfect unity that the world will know that you sent me and that you love them as much as you love me.*

5 MINUTES

Think about the following questions and how they might apply to your life.

• Who does Jesus say He's praying for in vs. 20? Who do you think is included in "all who will ever believe in me"?

- What does Jesus pray that we will be in vs. 21? What example does Jesus give for how we're supposed to be one? Who is our model for this?

- What do you think it means when Jesus says "as you are in me, Father, and I am in you. And may they be in us"?

- Jesus seems to be saying that all Christians should have the same unity that Jesus had with God the Father. (Remember, they're really ONE person!) How is that even possible? What do you think it means to be one with someone like God the Father and Jesus are one?

- According to the very end of vs. 21, why is it important that Christians are unified? What does this mean if we AREN'T unified?

3 MINUTES

Spend three minutes talking to God. Here are some things to talk to Him about today.

- In vs. 20 Jesus prays specifically for you. Think about that — Jesus prayed for you! Jesus — God who became a human. And He prayed for you. Spend some time thinking about it — that the God of the universe prayed for you by name. Spend some time thanking God for loving you and knowing you that well.

- Unity among Christians is a big deal. God wants us to love each other. To work together. To tell the truth to each other. To not be divided and argumentative. Pray that God would help you be unified with the Christ-followers around you. Pray for the times when that's really hard.

you can write your thoughts on the next page →

THOUGHTS

This space is here for you to jot down some thoughts, write out a prayer, draw a picture, or do whatever you want to help you remember your 10-minute moment.

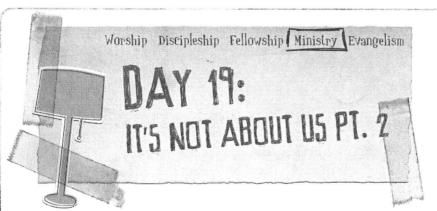

DAY 19:
IT'S NOT ABOUT US PT. 2

Back on day 8 we talked about how God isn't a genie that exists to fulfill our needs. But there's another way that it's "not about me." A lot of times we view people for what we can get out of them. We try to avoid people who make us uncomfortable or need something from us, and we spend time around people who make us feel valued or that we think we can get something out of. This is human nature. And it's not how God wants us to be.

2 MINUTES

Read the passages several times (as many times as you can in 2 minutes).

1 Corinthians 9:19
Even though I am a free man with no master, I have become a slave to all people to bring many to Christ.

Galatians 5:13-14
13For you have been called to live in freedom, my brothers and sisters. But don't use your freedom to satisfy your sinful nature. Instead, use your freedom to serve one another in love. 14For the whole law can be summed up in this one command: "Love your neighbor as yourself."

5 MINUTES

Think about the following questions and how they might apply to your life.

* In 1 Corinthians 9:19 what does Paul say he has become? What are some words that describe a servant's relationship

to a master? How would your life be different if those words were how you thought of your relationship with those around you?

- According to Paul, why does he make himself a slave to others?

- The Bible says elsewhere that we have freedom in Christ. In other words, our salvation doesn't come from following rules; it comes from what Jesus did for us. So theoretically we could do whatever we want. But what does Galatians 5:13 say we should do with our freedom?

- Why is freedom necessary to serve in love? Can anyone be FORCED to love?

- Who are some people in your life that you're good at serving (putting their needs ahead of yours)? Who are some people that it's hard for you to serve?

- What's one way you can choose to serve ONE of those people today?

3 MINUTES

Spend three minutes talking to God. Here are some things to talk to Him about today.

- Serving others instead of ourselves is one of the hardest things in the world to do. Ask God to help you have a servant's heart. Pray that He would show you areas where He wants you to be more of a servant.

- Spend time praying for people in your life that you know need prayer. Ask God to show you how you can show them love today.

THOUGHTS

This space is here for you to jot down some thoughts, write out a prayer, draw a picture, or do whatever you want to help you remember your 10-minute moment.

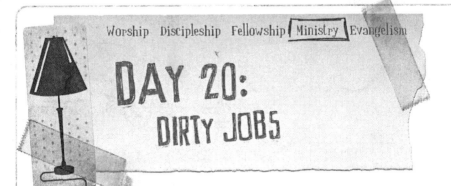

DAY 20:
DIRTY JOBS

One of the biggest signs of status in our culture is your job. The average career track starts in fast food (or if you're lucky, Starbucks) and then goes from there. The goal is to get higher and higher on the social/job ladder — and to never go back down. You don't see a lot of corporate executives cleaning bathrooms at McDonald's — which is what makes the following story about Jesus so remarkable.

2 MINUTES

Read the passage several times (as many times as you can in 2 minutes).

John 13:1-17

¹Before the Passover celebration, Jesus knew that his hour had come to leave this world and return to his Father. He had loved his disciples during his ministry on earth, and now he loved them to the very end. ²It was time for supper, and the devil had already prompted Judas, son of Simon Iscariot, to betray Jesus. ³Jesus knew that the Father had given him authority over everything and that he had come from God and would return to God. ⁴So he got up from the table, took off his robe, wrapped a towel around his waist, ⁵and poured water into a basin. Then he began to wash the disciples' feet, drying them with the towel he had around him.

⁶When Jesus came to Simon Peter, Peter said to him, "Lord, are you going to wash my feet?"

⁷Jesus replied, "You don't understand now what I am doing, but someday you will."

⁸"No," Peter protested, "you will never ever wash my feet!" Jesus replied, "Unless I wash you, you won't belong to me."

⁹Simon Peter exclaimed, "Then wash my hands and head as well, Lord, not just my feet!"

¹⁰Jesus replied, "A person who has bathed all over does not need to wash, except for the feet, to be entirely clean. And you disciples are clean, but not all of you." ¹¹For Jesus knew who would betray him. That is what he meant when he said, "Not all of you are clean."

¹²After washing their feet, he put on his robe again and sat down and asked, "Do you understand what I was doing? ¹³You call me 'Teacher' and 'Lord,' and you are right, because that's what I am. ¹⁴And since I, your Lord and Teacher, have washed your feet, you ought to wash each other's feet. ¹⁵I have given you an example to follow. Do as I have done to you. ¹⁶I tell you the truth, slaves are not greater than their master. Nor is the messenger more important than the one who sends the message. ¹⁷Now that you know these things, God will bless you for doing them."

5 MINUTES

Think about the following questions and how they might apply to your life.

- Read vs. 3 again. Does it seem weird to you that this verse is placed here? Why do you think the author of this book (John) put it in here?

- Why do you think it made Peter so uncomfortable to let Jesus wash his feet?

- Washing feet back then was a pretty nasty job — these guys had been walking on dirt roads in sandals all day long. Why do you think Jesus did it? What point was He making? (Check out vs. 14.)

- This moment was one of Jesus' last experiences with His disciples (He was crucified that night). Jesus wanted this to be one of the last things they remembered. Why is serving so important to Jesus?

- How do you think serving makes us different?

• Read vs. 17 again. What is one practical way you can serve someone today. (Don't wimp out! Make it something that's a little uncomfortable.)

3 MINUTES

Spend three minutes talking to God. Here are some things to talk to Him about today.

• As you prepare to radically serve someone today, pray that God would help you become the kind of person who WANTS to serve others. Ask God to change your heart so that you'd love the things that HE loves.

• Pray that God would use this service opportunity so that HE would be honored. Ask Him to help you not to serve in a way that tempts you to make serving about you.

• Think about how Jesus — who put the universe together — took time to wash the disciples' feet. Think about how He loves you the same way. Ask Him to help you to live in that love today — and to show it to others.

THOUGHTS

This space is here for you to jot down some thoughts, write out a prayer, draw a picture, or do whatever you want to help you remember your 10-minute moment.

DAY 21:
GOD'S PAINTINGS

Sometimes we approach our lives the way we might approach a painting. We feel this pressure to make our lives into a beautiful work of art, but a lot of times we feel like we're screwing it up. But this isn't exactly how the Bible sees us. Yes, it says that we're supposed to live our lives for God, but it ALSO says that our lives are ALREADY a masterpiece. It turns out that the painting of our life isn't in our hands after all — it's in God's hands. And we've been created to be a beautiful work of His art for the world around us.

2 MINUTES

Read the passage several times (as many times as you can in 2 minutes).

Ephesians 2:8-10
8God saved you by his grace when you believed. And you can't take credit for this; it is a gift from God. 9Salvation is not a reward for the good things we have done, so none of us can boast about it. 10For we are God's masterpiece. He has created us anew in Christ Jesus, so we can do the good things he planned for us long ago.

5 MINUTES

Think about the following questions and how they might apply to your life.

- What do you think it means to be God's masterpiece? What are some ways that we are like "God's painting"?

- Paintings don't paint themselves. They simply are what the artist designed them as. According to vs. 10, what kind of painting are we? (What has God created us to do?)

- If you WERE a painting, what kind of a painting do you think your life would be?

- What kind of painting do you think God sees you as?

Here's the deal — you were created to do good works. God has designed you that way. You don't have to try to BECOME someone who uses their gifts and abilities for the world around them — you already ARE that way. Your job is to learn how to act like it.

3 MINUTES

Spend three minutes talking to God. Here are some things to talk to Him about today.

- Talk to God today about what kind of masterpiece He intends for you to be. Specifically, ask God how He wants to use you to do great things for Him.

- If you have a hard time seeing yourself as special or beautiful or good, then spend some time asking God to help you see yourself like He does. Remember, you ARE a masterpiece — and God loves you a lot.

THOUGHTS

This space is here for you to jot down some thoughts, write out a prayer, draw a picture, or do whatever you want to help you remember your 10-minute moment.

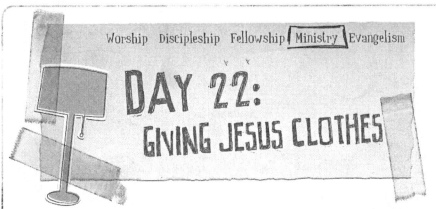

DAY 22:
GIVING JESUS CLOTHES

Imagine if tomorrow Jesus decided to come down to earth — but just for a day, and in disguise. He could be any one of the people you pass: the freshman getting picked on, the weird girl you avoid in class, the family member who gets on your nerves, or just one of the thousands of random, anonymous people you pass on a daily basis. Any one of them could be Jesus. If this were the case, would you treat people differently?

2 MINUTES

Read the passage several times (as many times as you can in 2 minutes).

Matthew 25:31-46

31"But when the Son of Man comes in his glory, and all the angels with him, then he will sit upon his glorious throne. 32All the nations will be gathered in his presence, and he will separate the people as a shepherd separates the sheep from the goats. 33He will place the sheep at his right hand and the goats at his left.

34"Then the King will say to those on his right, 'Come, you who are blessed by my Father, inherit the Kingdom prepared for you from the creation of the world. 35For I was hungry, and you fed me. I was thirsty, and you gave me a drink. I was a stranger, and you invited me into your home. 36I was naked, and you gave me clothing. I was sick, and you cared for me. I was in prison, and you visited me.'

37"Then these righteous ones will reply, 'Lord, when did we ever see you hungry and feed you? Or thirsty and give you something to drink? 38Or a stranger and show you hospitality? Or naked and give you clothing? 39When did we ever see you sick or in prison and visit you?'

⁴⁰"And the King will say, 'I tell you the truth, when you did it to one of the least of these my brothers and sisters, you were doing it to me!'

⁴¹"Then the King will turn to those on the left and say, 'Away with you, you cursed ones, into the eternal fire prepared for the devil and his demons. ⁴²For I was hungry, and you didn't feed me. I was thirsty, and you didn't give me a drink. ⁴³I was a stranger, and you didn't invite me into your home. I was naked, and you didn't give me clothing. I was sick and in prison, and you didn't visit me.'

⁴⁴"Then they will reply, 'Lord, when did we ever see you hungry or thirsty or a stranger or naked or sick or in prison, and not help you?'

⁴⁵ "And he will answer, 'I tell you the truth, when you refused to help the least of these my brothers and sisters, you were refusing to help me.'

⁴⁶"And they will go away into eternal punishment, but the righteous will go into eternal life."

5 MINUTES

Think about the following questions and how they might apply to your life.

- According to this passage, what is a characteristic of people who are followers of Jesus? What kind of people did they help (vs. 35)?

- According to vs. 40, when we help people less fortunate, who are we doing it for?

- Who are some of the people in your life that might be described as "the least of these"?

- Who are some of the people in the WORLD (whom you may or may not have met) who are hungry, poor, or naked? Are there ways you could help them?

- Why do you think Jesus says that helping people who are desperate is like "doing it to Him"? Why is it THAT important to Him?

3 MINUTES

Spend three minutes talking to God. Here are some things to talk to Him about today.

- God cares about people who are suffering. A LOT. There are at least 100 commands in the Old Testament alone to care for the poor. Spend time today asking God to show you the people who are poor, hurting, or in need of help.

- Currently almost half the people in the world — 3 billion people — live on less than $2.00 a day. Almost 30,000 children die each day due to poverty. An estimated 40 million people currently have AIDS. And the most financially blessed organization in the world — the American Church— still isn't doing as much as it could to help solve this crisis. Ask God what He would have you do about this. Tell Him you'll do whatever He wants to help "the least of these." Ask Him to break your heart for the poor people He loves so much.

THOUGHTS

This space is here for you to jot down some thoughts, write out a prayer, draw a picture, or do whatever you want to help you remember your 10-minute moment.

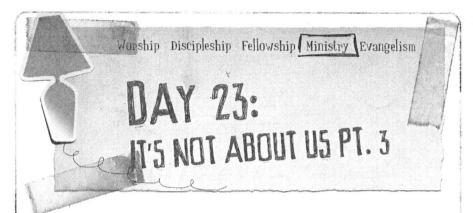

DAY 23:
IT'S NOT ABOUT US PT. 3

For yesterday's devotional we talked about some pretty hard-to-comprehend stuff: millions hungry, dying and diseased; a third of the world living in poverty. And then there are the people in our own lives who need help: the hurting at school, the abused and picked on, the lonely and depressed, the suicidal, the people who are ruining their lives with dangerous choices. What can we possibly do in the face of this much hurt?

2 MINUTES

Read the passage several times (as many times as you can in 2 minutes).

John 6:1-13

¹*After this, Jesus crossed over to the far side of the Sea of Galilee, also known as the Sea of Tiberias. ²A huge crowd kept following him wherever he went, because they saw his miraculous signs as he healed the sick. ³Then Jesus climbed a hill and sat down with his disciples around him. ⁴(It was nearly time for the Jewish Passover celebration.) ⁵Jesus soon saw a huge crowd of people coming to look for him. Turning to Philip, he asked, "Where can we buy bread to feed all these people?" ⁶He was testing Philip, for he already knew what he was going to do.*

⁷*Philip replied, "Even if we worked for months, we wouldn't have enough money to feed them!"*

⁸*Then Andrew, Simon Peter's brother, spoke up. ⁹"There's a young boy here with five barley loaves and two fish. But what good is that with this huge crowd?"*

¹⁰*"Tell everyone to sit down," Jesus said. So they all sat down on*

the grassy slopes. (The men alone numbered about 5,000.) [11]Then Jesus took the loaves, gave thanks to God, and distributed them to the people. Afterward he did the same with the fish. And they all ate as much as they wanted. [12]After everyone was full, Jesus told his disciples, "Now gather the leftovers, so that nothing is wasted." [13]So they picked up the pieces and filled twelve baskets with scraps left by the people who had eaten from the five barley loaves.

5 MINUTES

Think about the following questions and how they might apply to your life.

- Why do you think that in vs. 5 Jesus asks Phillip how they are going to feed all the people? What do you think the right answer for Phillip might have been?

- The Bible tells us there were 5,000 men there, but with women and children there might have been as many as 15,000-20,000. So if you were Andrew, would you have told Jesus about the fish and loaves? (Keep in mind, Andrew didn't know the end of the story.)

- Did Jesus NEED the five loaves and two fish? If not, why did He use them?

- How are our gifts and abilities kind of like the five loaves and two fish?

- If God could use a boy's lunch to feed more than 15,000 people, what could He do with you? This isn't hypothetical. What's the biggest thing you could imagine God using you to do?

The truth is that it's not our ability that changes the world around us — it's God using our small acts of service for something amazing. A lot of times we think that if the world's going to change, it depends on us. But it's not about us. It's about God working through us. And when we offer our small gifts for Him, miracles happen.

3 MINUTES

Spend three minutes talking to God. Here are some things to talk to Him about today.

- Ask God today to open up your eyes to the giant plan He has for you. Tell Him that you want Him to use your small acts of service — loving people, using your gifts and abilities for Him — to do a miracle in the world.

- Thank God for letting you be a part of His plan to change the world.

THOUGHTS

This space is here for you to jot down some thoughts, write out a prayer, draw a picture, or do whatever you want to help you remember your 10-minute moment.

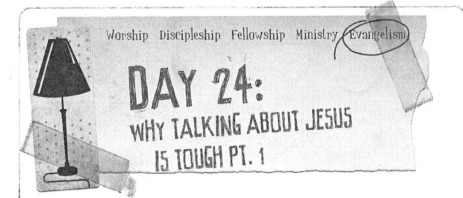

DAY 24:
WHY TALKING ABOUT JESUS IS TOUGH PT. 1

Lately, it seems like almost everyone is okay with talking about Jesus. He's on T-shirts (as a homeboy), He's the focus of best-selling books — both Christians and non-Christians alike and nearly everyone likes the fact that He cared about the poor and sick. To kind of quote the movie "Zoolander," Jesus is so hot right now. Or at least SOME things about Jesus are. But there are other things about Jesus that people don't like talking much about at all — like what He says in the verse below...

2 MINUTES

Read the passage several times (as many times as you can in 2 minutes).

John 14:6-11
6Jesus told him, "I am the way, the truth, and the life. No one can come to the Father except through me. 7If you had really known me, you would know who my Father is. From now on, you do know him and have seen him!"

8Philip said, "Lord, show us the Father, and we will be satisfied."

9Jesus replied, "Have I been with you all this time, Philip, and yet you still don't know who I am? Anyone who has seen me has seen the Father! So why are you asking me to show him to you? 10Don't you believe that I am in the Father and the Father is in me? The words I speak are not my own, but my Father who lives in me does his work through me. 11Just believe that I am in the Father and the Father is in me. Or at least believe because of the work you have seen me do.

5 MINUTES

Think about the following questions and how they might apply to your life.

- Who is the Father in vs. 6? How does Jesus say people can be in relationship with the Father?

- What do you think non-Christians see Jesus as? What did Jesus claim to be?

- One of the most popular thoughts today is that there are many paths to God. What does this passage — specifically vs. 6 — say about that?

- This passage — especially vs. 6 — is one of the most controversial statements Jesus ever made, and even today it upsets people. Why do you think that is?

- How do you feel about what Jesus says in this passage? Is it easy to accept, or do you have a hard time with it?

- We live in a world that tends to say "there's no ONE way," but that all ways are equally okay. But this isn't what Jesus says. He says He is THE way. And while we always want to approach people in love, there's no getting around the fact that Jesus' claim is going to make people upset. And this is one of the reasons why telling people about Jesus is tough.

3 MINUTES

Spend three minutes talking to God. Here are some things to talk to Him about today.

- As you pray today thank Jesus for restoring our relationship with God. Ask Him for courage in telling other people about Him. Specifically, pray for people you know who need to hear about Jesus. Pray that God would give you a loving way to tell others about Him.

THOUGHTS

This space is here for you to jot down some thoughts, write out a prayer, draw a picture, or do whatever you want to help you remember your 10-minute moment.

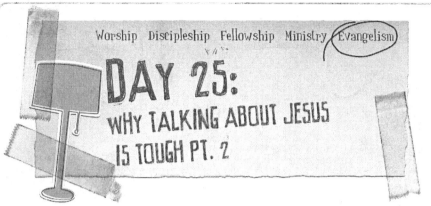

DAY 25:
WHY TALKING ABOUT JESUS IS TOUGH PT. 2

We talked yesterday about how Jesus' claim of being "the way, the truth, and the life" puts Him in direct conflict with a world that says "all ways work." Because of this, and a bunch of other reasons, telling people about Jesus is really tough — actually a lot of the time it's downright terrifying! But if you feel that way, you're not alone.

2 MINUTES

Read the passage several times (as many times as you can in 2 minutes).

2 Timothy 1:7-8
7For God has not given us a spirit of fear and timidity, but of power, love, and self-discipline.

8So never be ashamed to tell others about our Lord. And don't be ashamed of me, either, even though I'm in prison for him. With the strength God gives you, be ready to suffer with me for the sake of the Good News.

2 Timothy 1:12
That is why I am suffering here in prison. But I am not ashamed of it, for I know the one in whom I trust, and I am sure that he is able to guard what I have entrusted to him until the day of his return.

2 Timothy 1:15-16
15As you know, everyone from the province of Asia has deserted me—even Phygelus and Hermogenes.

16May the Lord show special kindness to Onesiphorus and all his family because he often visited and encouraged me. He was never ashamed of me because I was in chains.

5 MINUTES

Think about the following questions and how they might apply to your life.

- According to vs. 7 what kind of spirit has God NOT given us?

- What kind of spirit HAS He given us? What do these three things have to do with evangelism?

- Paul is writing this letter to a young guy (probably in his 20s) named Timothy who was the pastor of a church in Ephesus. Based on Paul's words in these verses, what do you think Timothy was struggling with?

- A lot of the times telling people about Jesus involves a lot of fear. What are some of the things we're afraid of?

3 MINUTES

Spend three minutes talking to God. Here are some things to talk to Him about today.

- Talk to God about people in your life that you know need to hear about Jesus. Ask Him to help you know when is the right time to say something and to know the words to say.

- It's normal to be scared when it comes to telling people we know about Jesus. Timothy was a PASTOR and he was so scared that Paul had to encourage him a half-dozen times in one chapter! Being a Christian isn't about not feeling fear; it's about not responding to it. Ask God to help you face whatever fears you're feeling when you think about sharing Jesus with someone.

- Spend some time praying for the other stuff going on in your life. Maybe it's family stuff or school or friends. Remember that God always wants us to talk with Him about the stuff we're going through.

THOUGHTS

This space is here for you to jot down some thoughts, write out a prayer, draw a picture, or do whatever you want to help you remember your 10-minute moment.

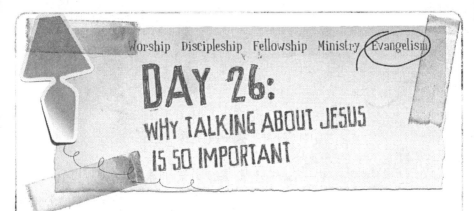

DAY 26:
WHY TALKING ABOUT JESUS IS SO IMPORTANT

The last two days we've talked a lot about how HARD it is to tell people about Jesus — and it's true that it's scary. But it's also so incredibly important. This verse below explains why.

2 MINUTES

Read the passage several times (as many times as you can in 2 minutes).

John 10:10-15
10"The thief's purpose is to steal and kill and destroy. My purpose is to give them a rich and satisfying life.

11"I am the good shepherd. The good shepherd sacrifices his life for the sheep. 12A hired hand will run when he sees a wolf coming. He will abandon the sheep because they don't belong to him and he isn't their shepherd. And so the wolf attacks them and scatters the flock. 13The hired hand runs away because he's working only for the money and doesn't really care about the sheep.

14"I am the good shepherd; I know my own sheep, and they know me, 15just as my Father knows me and I know the Father. So I sacrifice my life for the sheep."

5 MINUTES

Think about the following questions and how they might apply to your life.

* What does Jesus refer to Himself as in vs. 11? What do you think that means — how is Jesus like a shepherd? If Jesus is the shepherd, what does that make us?

- According to vs. 12-15, how is Jesus a good shepherd?

- Who do you think is the thief in vs. 11 and the wolf in vs. 12? (Hint: He's the same guy that was the lion from a couple weeks ago.)

- Can you see ways that people you know who aren't Christians are like unprotected sheep? What are some of the ways that Satan is trying to destroy them?

- Considering all of this, why is it so important to talk about Jesus?

3 MINUTES

Spend three minutes talking to God. Here are some things to talk to Him about today.

- Think about some people in your life who need to be in relationship with Jesus. The Bible says that Satan wants to do everything he can to destroy them. Pray that God would protect these people from the enemy's lies/attacks. Ask God to open their hearts to the truth of who He (God) is.

- Ask God to show you ways you can live out Jesus' love to these people today. Ask Him to help you to see people today the way He sees them.

- We don't think a lot about Satan and Jesus and sheep and stuff, and that's normal. But it's not okay for us to stay that way. Ask that God would over time help you to see the world as it really is.

- Thank God for loving you and loving the world around you. Talk to Him for a little about whatever's on your mind today.

you can write your thoughts ⟶
on the next page

THOUGHTS

This space is here for you to jot down some thoughts, write out a prayer, draw a picture, or do whatever you want to help you remember your 10-minute moment.

DAY 27:
JESUS LOVES ME

John 3:16 — it's one of the most famous verses in the Bible. And for some of us it's become so familiar we aren't really affected by it anymore — which is why today's time with God is all about that verse. So whether this is the first time you've read this verse or the 4,000th time, today we're just going to focus on making it feel like the first time. Before you start ask God to speak to you through this verse.

2 MINUTES

Read the passage several times (as many times as you can in 2 minutes).

John 3:16
For God loved the world so much that he gave his one and only Son, so that everyone who believes in him will not perish but have eternal life.

5 MINUTES

No questions today – just some thoughts to help this verse come alive:

- For God: The Milky Way galaxy alone is made up of approximately 400 billion stars and there are hundreds of billions of galaxies in the universe.

- so loved: And yet God says He knows the number of hairs on every person's head … and that He made each of us individually in our moms' wombs.

- the world: There are more than 6 billion people on this planet. The average person knows approximately 250 of them by name — less than a millionth of a percent. God knows them all. He feels their pain, questions, suffering, and sin.

- His one and only Son: God became human and died so we wouldn't have to live without Him for eternity.

- everyone who believes: All it takes is to believe God is who He says and that He did what the Bible says.

3 MINUTES

Spend three minutes talking to God. Here are some things to talk to Him about today.

- What stood out to you as you read through this? Pray about that.

THOUGHTS

This space is here for you to jot down some thoughts, write out a prayer, draw a picture, or do whatever you want to help you remember your 10-minute moment.

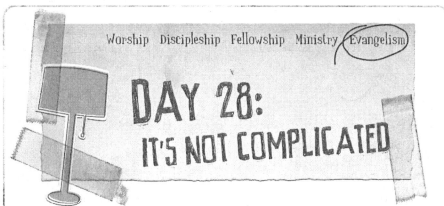

DAY 28:
IT'S NOT COMPLICATED

Sometimes Christians are afraid of telling people about Jesus because it seems so ... so ... COMPLICATED! I mean, what if you leave out a crucial detail? But it doesn't have to be hard. The discussion questions today will talk about basic things that people should know to accept Jesus. This isn't some kind of formula or checklist — just a way of helping you think through the important points.

2 MINUTES

Read the passage several times (as many times as you can in 2 minutes).

Romans 5:6-11
6When we were utterly helpless, Christ came at just the right time and died for us sinners. 7Now, most people would not be willing to die for an upright person, though someone might perhaps be willing to die for a person who is especially good. 8But God showed his great love for us by sending Christ to die for us while we were still sinners. 9And since we have been made right in God's sight by the blood of Christ, he will certainly save us from God's condemnation. 10For since our friendship with God was restored by the death of his Son while we were still his enemies, we will certainly be saved through the life of his Son. 11So now we can rejoice in our wonderful new relationship with God because our Lord Jesus Christ has made us friends of God.

Think about the following questions and how they might apply to your life.

- What does vs. 6 say we were before we became Christ-followers?

    ○ 1st big idea: Something's gone wrong. Humanity in general— and each of us individually — is broken because of sin. We're selfish and hurtful and none of us lives up to the standard of who we know we're supposed to be. This brokenness has separated us from God.

- What does vs. 8 say God did?

    ○ 2nd big idea: Jesus came for us. Rather than let us stay separated from Him, God became a human being. He refused to let us die without a chance to be reconnected to God.

- What does vs. 9 say happened because of Jesus' blood?

    ○ 3rd big idea: Jesus' dying and then coming back to life can fix us. Our brokenness — the Bible calls it sin — that separated us from God can be removed. Jesus makes it possible for us to not be separated from God anymore.

- What does vs. 11 say we have now because of what Jesus did?

    ○ 4th big idea: By believing in Jesus, we can live reconnected to God. More than that, it says we become "friends of God." Friends! Pretty incredible.

That's it. Just think of it like a story. We were broken and alone. Jesus didn't leave us alone. Through what He did we can be friends with God.

3 MINUTES

Spend three minutes talking to God. Here are some things to talk to Him about today.

- Pray for the people in your life who need Jesus. Pray that God would give you the chance to tell them about what Jesus did. Remember, these conversations with people normally happen gradually. You don't have to dump it on them all at once.

THOUGHTS

This space is here for you to jot down some thoughts, write out a prayer, draw a picture, or do whatever you want to help you remember your 10-minute moment.

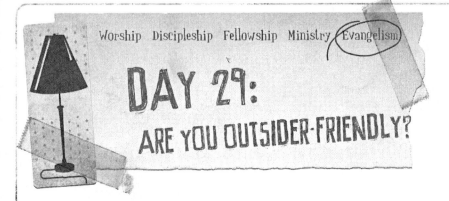

DAY 29:
ARE YOU OUTSIDER-FRIENDLY?

We've spent a lot of time before talking about the benefit of doing life with other Christ-followers. But there's one danger that can come from this: We get so comfortable hanging out with each other, we become closed off to the people around us who need Jesus.

2 MINUTES

Read the passage several times (as many times as you can in 2 minutes).

Luke 5:27-32

27Later, as Jesus left the town, he saw a tax collector named Levi sitting at his tax collector's booth. "Follow me and be my disciple," Jesus said to him. 28So Levi got up, left everything, and followed him.

29Later, Levi held a banquet in his home with Jesus as the guest of honor. Many of Levi's fellow tax collectors and other guests also ate with them. 30But the Pharisees and their teachers of religious law complained bitterly to Jesus' disciples, "Why do you eat and drink with such scum?"

31Jesus answered them, "Healthy people don't need a doctor—sick people do. 32I have come to call not those who think they are righteous, but those who know they are sinners and need to repent."

5 MINUTES

Think about the following questions and how they might apply to your life.

- Tax collectors were among the most hated people in Jesus' day, yet Jesus asks one of them — Levi — to be one of His 12 closest followers. Why do you think Jesus did this?

- Think about the attitude of the Pharisees (the religious people) in this story. How do you think their attitude made outsiders — like the tax collectors — feel about God?

- What does your life make other people think about God? Do people around you see an accepting God or a mean, distant, judgmental God?

- How does Jesus respond when the Pharisees call Jesus out for hanging with "scum"?

- Would you feel uncomfortable inviting someone who doesn't know Jesus to hang out with your Christian friends? Would they feel uncomfortable? If so, why?

- Would your small group, youth group, or circle of Christian friends be seen by outsiders as a safe and inviting group of people to be around? If your answer is yes, ARE there any actual non-Christians who are around your Christian circle? If not, why not?

3 MINUTES

Spend three minutes talking to God. Here are some things to talk to Him about today.

- Pray that God would make your group of Christ-following friends inviting, attractive examples of what a Christ-follower should look like.

- Are there people in your life that might not go to church but that you could invite to hang out with you and others who love Jesus? If so, pray that God would help you see opportunities to invite your non-Christian friends into your Christian friend circle.

THOUGHTS

This space is here for you to jot down some thoughts, write out a prayer, draw a picture, or do whatever you want to help you remember your 10-minute moment.

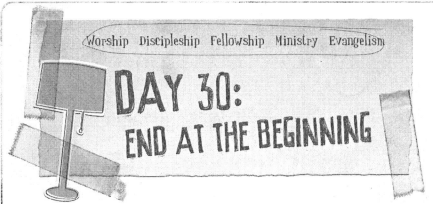

DAY 30:
END AT THE BEGINNING

Back at day 1 we said that there was no dividing line between God-stuff and non-God-stuff. And really that's what this entire 30-day devotional has been about — being completely plugged in to the presence of God. He wants us to live for Him (worship) in every way: with our hearts and mind (discipleship); by doing life with other Christ-followers (fellowship); by living life for Him and others instead of ourselves (ministry); and by doing everything we can to help people start a relationship with Jesus (evangelism). These five purposes are what life is all about. When we do all five we are becoming completely plugged in to God's presence. We are realizing that everything is spiritual and living a life as close as possible to what He intends for us. When we do that, God's power flows through us, and the world changes.

2 MINUTES

Read the passage several times (as many times as you can in 2 minutes).

Colossians 3:17
And whatever you do or say, do it as a representative of the Lord Jesus, giving thanks through him to God the Father.

5 MINUTES

Think about the following questions and how they might apply to your life.

* This is the verse we read on day 1. Look back at your notes from day 1. Does this verse look any different to you now than it did then? If so, what's changed? What's one way

over the last month that God has challenged you to worship Him in everything you do?

- What is an area of your life where you feel God is challenging you to let go of your way, and worship Him? How can you ask other Christ-followers to help you with that?

3 MINUTES

Spend three minutes talking to God. Here are some things to talk to Him about today.

- Thank God for any changes you see in your life from the last week.

- Ask God for His help with anything you know He's still speaking to you about.

- Pray that God would show you His plan for your life. This might happen during your prayer time today, but it might not. That's okay. The key is to keep praying daily that God would help you to stay plugged in to His plan. Ask Him for help in doing that. Ask Him to help you remember that He loves you even when you mess up.

- Pray over the next 24 hours of your life. Ask God to help you see where He wants to use you.

THOUGHTS

This space is here for you to jot down some thoughts, write out a prayer, draw a picture, or do whatever you want to help you remember your 10-minute moment.